Purses, Pearls & Pumps

Purses, Pearls & Pumps

Straight Talk About Women & Finances

BONITA VINSON, Ph.D.

VC
PUBLISHING
2013

Purses, Pearls & Pumps: Straight talk about women and finances
Copyright © 2013, Bonita Vinson, Ph.D.

This book is written to provide accurate and authoritative information with regard to the subject matter covered. This information is given with the understanding that Bonita Vinson is not engaged in rendering legal, accounting or other professional advice. Because the details of your personal financial situation are fact dependent, you should additionally seek the services of a competent professional.

Unless otherwise indicated, all Scripture quotations are taken from the Holy Bible, New Living Translation, copyright © 1996, 2004, 2007 by Tyndale House Foundation. Used by permission of Tyndale House Publishers, Inc., Carol Stream, Illinois 60188. All rights reserved.

ISBN: 978-0-9894976-6-4

Printed in the United States of America

Book Design by Bradley Vinson

Second Edition

For Alanna

— CONTENTS —

In recent generations we have lavished ourselves in luxuries we cannot afford. Most of us have stockpiled name-brand purses, luxurious jewelry, and enough name-brand shoes to outfit an army. *Purses, Pearls & Pumps* is an honest and frank conversation with women about our financial condition and how to improve it. I have used stories from my own personal life, financial struggles and victories—and those of women I have coached—and I hope any woman who reads this book will take an in-depth look at her own financial condition and be inspired to make it better.

My approach to having a conversation with women about this necessary but delicate topic is to first present the facts. I discuss factual information about the history of debt in the American culture, and how it has affected our families and us in particular. But, don't worry. You are not alone! Statistics show staggering numbers of women from all walks of life struggling with the same financial issues whether single, married, or a single mom.

Early on, I identify the *Marketing Machine*, as I call it, whose purpose is to strip us of our money and suggest what we can do to defeat it. I even discuss the role of family, both in the process to take our money and in the process of recapturing a stable financial position in life.

Then I show you a time-tested, proven method of combating your financial woes and bringing them under control so that you can be on your way to financial freedom. I use stories from my own life and become transparent in sharing my failures and successes with you in the hope that they will inspire you to victorious living. My life of financial ruin to financial peace speaks loudly throughout the pages, but I could no longer sit idly by and watch women continue to suffer financially without offering some form of hope.

This book provides hope to women who are struggling with their individual or family financial situation. At any starting point, women can align themselves with this book from where they are financially and gain hope. They will walk away with examples and guidance on how to improve their financial situation. Women of all income brackets, ages, and walks of life have something to gain from reading and engaging in this book.

My husband, Bradley Vinson, inspired me as he began to write and receive great feedback about the need for his book, *Men, Get Real With Your Finances...It Takes More Than Money To Win*. Many of the voices that motivated him to author his book asked for a female companion book for the woman in their lives (i.e. wife, mother, daughter, sister). And, because we are involved together in the ministry to deliver a faith-based approach to personal finances, it only seemed natural that I accept the challenge. It turned out not to be a challenge at all, but more of a calling to give a female voice to this important topic. The book almost wrote itself once I allowed the voice to speak from my truth and the truth of many of the women I have counseled, coached and taught. It just had to be.

I invite you to join me on the journey to a new outlook on financial freedom that will set you free from the fear of conquering your financial discontentment. Anyone can be successful using the methods I present in the pages that follow. It will take a lot of hard work and sacrifice. I will not offer you financial products, pyramid schemes or some other money-depleting package. You can get started with this book, a pad of paper and a pencil. The rest is up to you!

In *Men, Get Real With Your Finances...It Takes More Than Money to Win*, Bradley speaks candidly to men about the influence they have over their family's financial condition. If you have a spouse, brother, uncle, friend, or coworker, you will want to make sure that they have a copy of his book. It is uplifting and empowering! It helps men see themselves and their role in an entirely different light. They will gain insight, knowledge and power to start or strengthen a victorious financial path and declare a new financial legacy for themselves and their families.

CHAPTER 1

Our Financial Condition

America's Financial Condition

Living paycheck-to-paycheck, mounting debt, payday loans, foreclosure, bankruptcy, depleted savings, no savings, financial ruin, no future, and broke/busted/disgusted: these are terms we have all heard or said. They apply to someone you know or to your own life. Many Americans don't know how they got into their financial mess or how to get out of it. As a financial teacher, empowerment speaker and financial coach, I've heard too many stories of people who are in trouble with money, on the brink of divorce, or just plain giving up on life because they see no way out of the financial crisis they find themselves in. They don't realize that they are not alone. In America today, the average household income is $49,777 and the average household debt is $70,000 (US Census Bureau). That means most Americans live beyond their means. In fact, nearly 70% of households live paycheck to paycheck (American Payroll Association). The research shows increasing percentages of upper income families live paycheck to paycheck as well. This means that income level is not a predictor of household debt level. Behavior is.

The condition of living life from paycheck to paycheck has become so normal in U.S. culture that we have accepted it as a way of life. For most Americans, we spend our paycheck before it hits the bank and if there is some left over we find ways to make it disappear before the next one comes. This vicious cycle causes undue stress on our lives, marriages, workplaces, and health. This was not the way our lives were meant to be lived; yet, we not only buy into this as a normal way of life, we are reluctant to accept that there are productive alternatives that allow us to live a successful, happy, independent, and victorious life.

In my years of financial empowerment teaching and coaching, I have come to realize that income level does not affect this condition. I have seen people with barrels full of money (seemingly) living on the brink of financial ruin; I have also seen individuals with low, fixed incomes in the same condition. In contrast, I have seen families from both of these types rise up from ruin to financial empowerment, take control of their financial destiny and live victoriously. What does matter is not a higher income level, but what you do with the money you have. Behavior matters.

As humans we are created with free will and have the ability to design, accept, or conquer our financial lives. We can choose to be part of the statistics mentioned above or we can be different and take our financial future on a course that can work wonders for us in the short-term and long-term. As creatures of habit, once we accept the paycheck-to-paycheck way of living, we adopt all of the tenets offered by it as our own.

We spend so many years in a financial cycle of earning, spending and borrowing that we never really question what we are doing to our financial future based on what the crowd is doing. It's mostly a subconscious act, but we do it nonetheless. After many years of borrowing money credit cards, car loans, mortgages, signature loans, family/friends, no significant savings, and income levels that either stay the same or decline—when cost of inflation is factored in—Americans become convinced that this is the cycle we must live in and that there is no alternative to it. It becomes our way of life; just the way things ought to be.

My husband Bradley is the leader of our team—Team Vinson—and he calls this the *Cycle of Hopelessness*—the belief that life will not get any better, so one might as well join the crowd in this endless Cycle. It's a Cycle that never ends and perpetuates itself generation after generation. In our ignorance, we teach our children detrimental financial lessons that cause them to enter the Cycle and accept the same mindset. We must have debt, live in debt and die with loads of debt. A relative told me when I was a teenager, "you will always owe someone, so you might as well get what you can get and just hope you'll pay it off before you die." I didn't know why then, but I rejected that notion. After gaining greater financial insight I now know that the statement is actually true, but only if one accepts this as the truth. I was unaware that I was in the Cycle of Hopelessness, but I was aware that I was not doomed to repeat it; nor are you. You have the power to end the Cycle today. If you follow my guidance, you will gain knowledge and equip yourself with the power to win financially.

In Chapter 5 we will discuss several financial myths, why they are not true and what you can do to live in the truth instead of continuing to perpetuate myths. What is interesting to me are the reasons and excuses people adopt to justify their bad financial habits. Some of them come from lies you have been told about your financial condition or expectations. Some of them come from what popular culture teaches you about money and finances. And some stem from behaviors you witnessed as a child and in your youth that remain with you and will not leave you until you dismiss them from your lives.

Regardless of what your problem is with money, there is a fix, not a quick fix, but a fix nonetheless. You can choose to remain in financial bondage or you can choose to break free. It really is bondage when you are in an endless Cycle and can't find your way out. It's bondage when the weight of the financial burden and financial stress is so heavy that you can feel its weight on your shoulders, weighing you down. It's bondage when you feel like your hands are chained at your feet so that you can't even raise yourself out of the situation. Now that's bondage!

Still, hope remains and the answer lies within you. Are you willing to admit that financial devastation may impact your life (or already has)? Are you willing to admit that your way of handling money has failed or needs improvement? Are you willing to subject yourself to a tried and proven method that does not require gimmicks to help you break free? And, if you do not have debt in your life are you willing to learn methods to help you increase your savings, allow you to give like never before and live victoriously?

You should be "sick and tired" by now of living the way you have been living, seeing results that are not different, living from paycheck-to-paycheck. You cannot continue to borrow your way out of financial bondage. It takes work, hard work, sacrificing luxuries and plenty of strength you don't know you have. There is a source that can give you the strength you need to combat financial bondage based on some pretty cool principles that have been around for centuries.

Financial empowerment is not rocket science. It is a roadmap. If you have a roadmap to follow it can be an easy journey out of financial bondage to financial freedom. If you are ready, I have just the roadmap for you. Now is your time! The journey is calling you (or calling you back). You hold the keys to your financial future in your hands (and your spouse's if you are married). The process has been proven over and over as people break the financial Cycle of more debt and less savings and come to know how to break financial bondage and live victorious financial lives. I want to extend a challenge to you to allow the teachings in this book to help you break free and become victorious! Are you ready for the challenge?

Financial Condition of Women in America

While the numbers, statistics and realities discussed in the previous section are astounding, they are even more astounding when we talk about the financial condition of women in America. Because of many factors including low-earning occupations, women still earn only 77 cents for every dollar men earn. Combine this with our need to purchase things and the outlook is bleak.

Female Consumerism

It's no secret. Women love to shop and spend money. Yes, me too! I'm not sure if it's innate or if it is a behavior we learn after many years of grooming and societal expectations. This book is not really focused on the psychological nature vs. nurture debate, but it is written to address the behaviors that have us in financial trouble, and then offer an escape and a new way of thinking. I suspect, however, that we have learned to purchase things that enhance our lifestyle and for our children instead of having the power over purchase as an innate function.

Women Purchase Differently

As women, we make different purchases than men. We tend to purchase small-ticket items and make purchases more often whereas men tend to purchase large-ticket items less often. 2013 data from the US Bureau of Labor Statistics report on Consumer Expenditures shows this trend to be true. You may justify your spending because it is not a lot, but remember that it is possible to nickel-and-dime the money right out of your accounts. The men in your life tend to spend less money over time even though they purchase bigger ticket items than we. Ideally, you will curtail the household spending so that you can attend to other matters that require the attention of your finances.

Women engage in spending that satisfies a deeply seeded emotion that continues from childhood. And afterwards, we feel guilty for having made the purchases. Although we realize that the stuff we buy does not rectify what is deficient in our lives, we continue the same Cycle over and over. Countless women have shared with me that they engage in emotional spending. I used to do the same thing. I got mad at hubby, felt badly, went shopping, and felt better until I arrived home. It was a never-ending Cycle over and over again.

Unlike their male counterparts, women tend to buy items they never or rarely use. I can't tell you how many of my friends are guilty of this. Before I go any further, I must confess. I recently found a skirt in my closet that had never been worn, with the tag still on it. I was disgusted because I felt that I had wasted money on something I obviously did not need. The skirt had been in the closet so long that I forgot why I bought it in the first place, but I'm sure it was because it was on sale. The skirt was too small for me now!

On the other hand, I found a pair of slacks in Bradley's closet with tags on it. He recently purchased them and I had no idea he had not worn them. When I questioned him about the slacks he explained that he purchased them to wear to an event we attended, but had not tried them on in the store. When he put them on that night for the event he discovered they were too tight in the legs, took them off, and hung them up only to forget about them for two months. His purpose of the purchase was totally different from mine. The purchase served a purpose in his mind whereas finding something on sale that could be used later was my reasoning.

Do you see how easy it can be to deceive yourself into believing that a purchase is necessary when it really is not? If you are like I used to be, you probably have many items in your closet(s) with tags on them hoping to fit in them or have the perfect matching pieces one day.

This behavior must stop if you want to win financially! I cannot stress this enough. It really must stop, immediately!

Women are more likely to hoard pop-culture items. The need to be in style is real. Something happens (I believe subconsciously) when you make purchases (clothes, shoes, accessories, vehicles, homes, etc.) just because it is the latest thing. You will not want to admit this—no one does. But it's the truth nevertheless. You have to control your desire to be in possession of the latest and greatest items. I have my category of stuff that makes me feel better and so do you.

Think about what category of stuff is for you. It doesn't matter how much "the stuff" costs or what financial sacrifice you must make; all you know is you have to have what you desire. If the item is small enough you will go to great lengths to ensure that you have more and more of them and may even hide them in the trunk of the car or the closet.

The most common item is shoes. I hear women talking all the time about how they can't help but add more shoes to their collection. The more they have, the better they think they look and feel. The truth is that if you only had one pair of shoes you would still look the same. Think about what you are really purchasing the shoes for—approval from other people. It pains me to know that you purchase shoes on credit and/or purchase shoes well beyond your means—adding debt and sacrificing more important financial goals—for the sake of having someone else look at you with approval.

Don't get me wrong, I want you to have some stuff, but more importantly, I want you to have your financial life in order so that when you get stuff, you can really afford the stuff you get. Afford means you can make the purchase with cash, and does not take away from your short- or long-term financial goals. You will have plenty of opportunities later to make sound, relevant purchases of stuff that make sense in your new financial life.

We need to let go of our inner desire to please others, which is where most of our purchases come from. Outside of reasonable accommodation, food, transportation and clothing, there isn't anything else that should be a priority for our lives while we climb our way out of debt and change poor money management behavior. Everything else can wait—everything. The process I will show you will allow you to slowly add "stuff" to your spending allowances as you save and eliminate debt.

Women Borrow, Men Not As Much

Another difference between men and women is that we are more likely to borrow/use credit for purchases although we are more likely to pay it back or make payments. Well, it doesn't matter. The behavior can be the same whether we spend cash or put it on credit. The problem comes in when we fall for the bargain shopping and percentage-off for using credit. We have become more and more notorious for this behavior. We trick ourselves into thinking that we have out-bargained the retailer. Believe me, they are in business because they make profit. And yes, maybe we did not pay full price, but we didn't win at the game. Retail items are marked up so much that unless we get it for free and pay cash, the retailer still makes a profit.

Need a Good Wrangling—Cause We Won't Go Down Easy

As women, we are so out of control with spending that someone needs to wrangle us back in and make us stop. The fact that you are reading this right now means you desire to be told that very thing. You will not regret stepping forward and having the courage to admit that a problem exists and that you need to know something new to fix it. Congratulations!

I remember when Bradley and I decided enough was enough; we had to make some drastic changes to our behavior because we were "sick and tired." As we looked at what we were spending we knew we had to make adjustments or we would not win. We would continue to operate in the Cycle of Hopelessness. Without saying anything to each other and in our own time we each made commitments to drop some things that were eating up our take-home pay.

Bradley knew that although he was not eating up our income buying lunch every day, he would make several trips to the local big-box retail store's $5 movie bin each week. And any technology he could find, he had to have it, justifying it because of his side business. His "enough" moment caused him to promise he would buy no more technology and watch only the movies he already owned until we became debt free. He also cut the cable TV down to the basic level saving us over $150 per month, but we signed up for the mail order movie plan for a fraction of the cost. This was his commitment. It came to him over time and through prayer and gentle communication with each other. I did not force these sacrifices on him. I did not ask him to do it. We agreed and swore that we would do whatever it took to get out of debt.

As for me, I was not going down without a fight. But after a little while, as the family budgeter, I realized I was spending far too much on personal care. I wasn't willing to give up my weekly visits to the hair and nail salons, beauty products, accessories, and everything else I felt it took to make me look good. I was spending $300 per month. What could you do with an extra $300 per month?

I decided to get my hair done every other week and do my nails at home to curtail expenses. I still looked and felt great! That still was not enough money cut from the budget, so I decided to only get my relaxer done at the shop and do my own hair the other four weeks. After about two years, I chose to wear my hair natural without texture altering chemicals.

Then I realized that shopping was the biggest, personal item I had. I don't mean shopping for groceries or necessities. When I realized this, I said to myself, "Stop it!" And I did. I threw away the Sunday newspaper sales circulars and stayed out of the malls, departments and discount stores. If it was not on my necessities list, I did not buy it! I did not intend for it to happen, but for two solid years I told myself this and it worked. I still can't believe it! I had thought it would take long to prove that I could exist without shopping. I'm surprised it didn't take longer. My entire attitude about going shopping and buying stuff is completely different now. But, so is my attitude about myself!

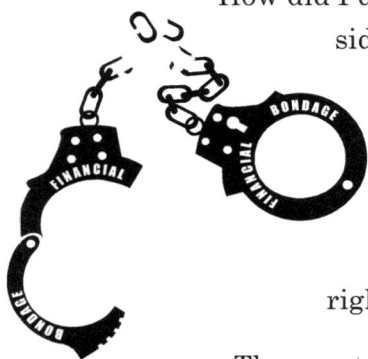

How did I do this? I imagined a balance. On one side was the life I was living—in financial bondage; on the other side was freedom from the bondage of debt. Each day, week, and month I had a choice. I asked myself which life I wanted. Ultimately, I made the right choice.

The most important lesson I learned was to stop living my life seeking the approval of others. Yes, I love it when someone compliments me, but unlike in the past, I no longer care what others think of me, my nails, my hair, shoes, dress, car or anything. If I can't save up and pay cash for it and if it takes away from future financial goals, then I don't need it. Sure, I desire a luxury car. The day you see me driving one will be the day you know I saved up and paid cash for it causing no financial burden on my family or my future.

What are you willing to do or change in order to win financially? I recognize that it is an emotionally difficult question to answer. At some point you will have to tell yourself to stop spending. You'll probably have to say it really loudly as you look in the mirror one day. Do it and be specific about what you are going to stop so that you can win. Make the commitment to yourself. Today is the best day to start.

Chapter 1 Take-Aways

List three insights you gained from this chapter.

1.

2.

3.

List three things you learned about yourself.

1.

2.

3.

List three behaviors/actions you will change and say why.

1.

2.

3.

CHAPTER 2

How Did We Get This Way?

Messages from Family

Believe it or not, most of us are in our financial condition due to messages we learned while growing up in our families. Think about it. How does the way you pay your bills compare to how you witnessed adults in your family paying bills? How do your shopping habits compare to how you saw women in your family shop (mainly your maternal role model)? How does your savings account mirror that of the women in your family? Do you even know? What about your debt load mirrors or mimics those who influenced you as a child or young adult? It's amazing to think about the influence familial patterns have on your own behavior. But, realize that we also have the same influence on the children and the young people in our lives.

One thing I have learned in my near half century on the planet is that there really is no way around our current condition. We can't go back and undo what we have done; we can't undo what others have done to us. We are where we are right now and we can't change anything prior to right now. We have the very hand of cards we have been dealt, so the best thing to do is to play the best hand we can.

Think of any card game. Once we understand the strategy of winning the game it is easier and more beneficial to play to win the game. When I was growing up, my older siblings would play card games—I mean the serious ones. Occasionally they would allow me to sit at the table or play a hand. It seemed like I would always lose or cause my team to lose because I did not understand the game—the strategy—well enough to win. The more I sat at the table of those with wisdom about how the game was played, listened to their stories, and made note of the strategies that caused each team to win or lose, I became better at the game. It took lots of practice and me walking away with tears in my eyes before I learned to play to win.

Strategy is the key component in the quest to win financially. We must learn the strategies needed to give us hope and the financial tools that can take us from our present situation to a new, hopeful and successful financial future. Thus far, you have employed strategies to get you to this point. If you are like I was, your strategy led to financial loss instead of gain. It led to confusion instead of purpose. It led to admitting the need for help instead of the power of providing assistance to those in need.

It is totally possible for us to cast away unproductive messages from society and others, keep successful messages, and develop new thoughts for our financial success from this point onward. Once we have investigated the old messages that did not help us win in the financial realm, we can choose to discard them. Be sure to re-equip your financial tool belt as you begin to discard tools that are not useful. Conversely, those successful financial tools we witnessed when we were younger should be adopted or kept in our financial toolkit. And finally, it does not matter where we begin, we all can learn something new that will equip us with a great strategy for moving forward on our trek to financial independence.

Purses, Pearls & Pumps outlines successful financial tools and a clear path to financial freedom if followed wholeheartedly. It will call for you to be sold out to the process for as long as the process takes. It will call for you to sacrifice and discard some unnecessary things for your success. It will cause you to say the most important and underused word in the English language— NO! You will have to say this to yourself and others along the way. It's a powerful word, and necessary in this process.

You have my permission to make unlimited use of this word as long as you are sold out to the process I outline and you have thought and prayed about how you might counteract reactions to your use of this word. Sometimes, the negative responses you will get will come from your spouse, children, family, friends, coworkers and even yourself. "No" can be a harsh word, especially when we have not had the discipline or courage to enforce it consistently.

When we were on our Journey to debt freedom I remember a time when I tried every trick in the book to convince my husband I needed a new (and financed) car. My Honda Civic was 8 or 10 years old and was not as reliable as it once was. It was a great car, truthfully. But after all, I worked hard and believed I had "earned" a nicer car. And for my position at work, I needed to impress the people who would visit or that I might transport from time to time. We first looked at Volvos, then Acuras, and then I realized they were all the same just with different luxury items on the inside. My tactics were successful. We settled on a $30,000 Honda Accord. And of course we got a great interest rate (wink, wink)!

Even though it felt good, the moment I drove into my driveway I had a sinking feeling in my gut. We were trying to eliminate debt, but instead we gained more. I was looking and feeling good on the road, but when the debt balance increased and as I looked at it each month I was not happy. Not happy about the purchase, and not about our financial condition that I justified. What messages did we send our teenaged children? That it's okay, normal and what one should do to get ahead in life? Could those messages be reversed? My husband and I vowed at that time that once we became debt free we would not borrow money again. And the workplace I thought I needed to impress with the new car was long gone by the time we were released from the bondage of debt.

The statement we frequently share with singles and couples alike about buying more stuff is "you don't have anything we want bad enough to go into debt for." Now, if we want something, we save up and pay cash for it. At the writing of this book, we have not had a credit card for at least 7 years. Nope. Not for travel (we travel all the time). Not for car rentals—they hit the debit card for a "hold" amount, but we are prepared for that. They can keep their designer purses. They can keep their cultured pearl necklaces, earrings and bracelets. They can keep their red-bottom shoes. And even though we can make payments without a problem, they can keep their luxury cars. We will not go into debt for anything. Not for anything! Never again!

I believe that this "sold-out" attitude is how we have been able to abstain from living in the bondage of debt and the Cycle of Hopelessness. It is this "sold-out" attitude that our children, family, and friends see us live every day of our lives. It is this "sold-out" attitude that allows us to sleep peacefully, travel, save for the future, and do whatever we want and are called to do. It is this "sold-out" attitude that allows us to support worthy causes, if we so desire, and give to our church. It is the "sold-out" attitude that has changed our family legacy forever!

We know our family and children are watching. Good! Please do not misunderstand; I am not boasting. We still have a long way to go on this Journey. I am using a very real story to demonstrate the power of family in the quest to financial freedom and the influence we have on future generations. I pray that my transparency resonates with you and motivates you to make changes in your life that will set you on a course to win financially and in the other areas of your life as well.

Messages from the Media

Credit, credit, credit. Debt, debt, debt. Low interest, no interest, zero-down, 84 months to pay, 90 days same as cash. Buy now, pay later. No credit, no problem. Save 10% now if you apply for The Card. With interest rates so low you can't afford not to buy.... You need the bigger, better, faster.... You'll be more beautiful if you just had... "They" will accept you if you just had....

If you are like me, these messages sound all too familiar. The desire, pressure, and entitlement to have the latest and greatest "whatever" and to have it right now at any cost is the genius behind the marketing campaigns you will find on any television or radio station, billboard, magazine, the Internet and social media outlets all over the world. They are very good at tapping into our inner need to feel loved, be accepted, and be able to boast. They are experts at telling us what we want, what we need, and how we will get it. They sell us on their products and services so well that we even tell and teach others that they need it in the same way.

Marketing Machines, as I call them, will go to any length to persuade us we need to continue to buy into debt or cause some other need in our lives to lack just to have whatever it is they sell (or we are not a whole person). They don't care about you, your family's well being, or whether your future is brighter or dimmer. They just want your money—all of it—and they will undercut, undermine, and have you undervalue yourself just to get it! If you think I am making this up, just try to open the Sunday paper without tearing open that insert of sales ads. There was a point in our debt freedom process where I realized I used to open the circular each Sunday with a pen or marker in hand so that I could mark all of the stuff I "needed" to buy.

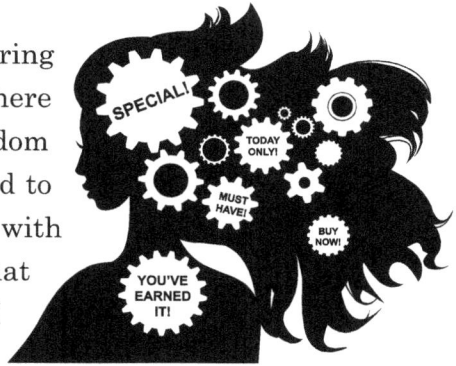

The truth is that I did not need to buy anything...really! But each week my habit was to canvass the circular and start my weekly trip to the malls, department and discount stores. After all, it was on sale and such a great buy! I was doing my family good deeds by catching things on sale wasn't I? Sure— believe that if you want to—except for the "other stuff" that always managed to catch my eye while I was out shopping. Lucky us! And, don't forget the pleasure I had when friends and colleagues inquired from where I got "it." I was proud to say that I "got it on sale" at whatever store.

I started to realize that a certain department store always has a one-day sale. What? Every other week? Really, self? When will you catch on that this is part of the *Marketing Machine* designed to pull the discretionary, unnamed (and sometimes obligated) money from your hands. I can still sing the tune to that one-day sale and even to this day it prompts a desire in me to go shopping. What a hook they had in my mouth!

Surely I was the only person who fell for it. As it turns out, the entire culture fell for this and other genius marketing ploys from the Marketing Machine designed to distract us and win our purchase power.

There is a science to product persuasion. Seriously. There are college professors who build their careers on understanding why you make purchases, what causes you to choose one product over another, what makes you choose to use your dollars on purchases versus savings, and what type of companies are more successful at getting you to spend your money. They are skillful at product placement of sugary cereals at your child's eye level, store lighting to flatter your skin tone, and using the scent of freshly baked cookies to lure you into the store. It is fascinating when I think about how the Marketing Machine contributed to my own financial demise and the power it had over my consumerism then as compared to now.

Each purchase you make fulfills at least a need—physiological, psychological, practical—and corporations pay to know what works, with whom, when, why and how. I told you there is a science to consumerism. From the colors, décor, architecture, smell, sound, and overall look and experience, scientists know what works for you. They know what makes you purchase more, less, faster, and slower. They design everything around the science of buying—from whom they choose to appear in advertisements and whom they choose to service us over the phone—to how, when or if they follow up with your purchase.

Remember that post-maintenance survey call you get? That's not really designed to find out how well their technician did; it's designed to give you one last good feeling that will stand out in your mind when the follow-up post cards come in the mail. You will refer to the "they care that much about me" phone call when triggered by the mailer, which will lead to your purchasing with them again.

That's why science is so important and necessary. Scientists are not just those who study biology, zoology, or the earth's crust. They also study one of the most fascinating beings of all times—the human being. Even if one becomes a business or psychology professor who researches the science of buying, the need for their expertise (not to mention companies who specialize in this) will always be sought after and paid for by corporations. The results of their research can be capitalized on and sifted down to a need rather than a want for you to purchase.

I own a travel agency, Vinson Creative Destinations. As a travel professional, I take a different look at travel products than I did as a consumer of travel only. I took a recent cruise with Bradley on the Disney Magic. We wrote part of this book and his on the cruise. A guided tour of the ship revealed some spectacular features of the ship. Believe it or not, your experience on the ship is a marketing tool used to get you to love it so much that you will want to purchase the experience over and over again.

I learned that from the moment you step on the ship you are sold an "experience" when they announce your family name as you enter the gangway to a captivating view into the Grand Entrance with its grand staircase, Chihouly grand chandelier, art deco theme and of course a statue of Captain Mickey. Adults and children alike are awestruck as they enter the vessel. We were too! It truly set the stage for all of the excitement in the days to come on the cruise. Now that the stage was set, dining, spa, character, and other experiences were great to exceptional. Who would not want to come back?

The Disney product is not by itself. Travel providers' main goal is for your "experience" to be such that you will want to purchase their product over and over and over again. This is why you see many exciting and cutting-edge features on newer versions of their products. If they are successful in their "experience" delivery then they win in the end with more sales and greater profit. Travel providers could care less if you choose to put the entire experience on credit and have it follow you home month after month, if you pay cash or have someone else purchase it for you. They just want the revenue.

Bradley and I have frequently traveled on cruise ships for years now through the "save up and pay for it" method. It works so well that we are able to enjoy our vacations free and clear of fear that they would follow us home on a credit card statement or empty bank account. This was our second cruise on the Disney Magic within six months. They sold us on the "experience!" Who knows where we will travel with the Disney product next, but we know for sure we will travel without debt!

And we know that we have more purchasing power by using a budget and paying cash than if we were to blindly use consumer debt hoping it would not follow us home. Our purchases are so much more purposeful, meaningful, and strategic.

Can you imagine the many slants corporations take in learning more about your spending patterns? It's amazing and never-ending! Just think about those rewards programs. You have the rewards cards in your wallet, purse or even on your keychain. They are tied to your email accounts, cell phone numbers, customer numbers and telephone numbers. And let's not forget that there is now an app that allows you to have these cards on your phone in case you don't want to carry them. You don't have to look for them—they can find you. When we re-boarded the Disney Magic after an onshore excursion, we presented our guest room keycard to security and still had to scan our thumbs for reentry into the ship. They have our thumbprints too! I wonder what the thumbprint information is used for!

Sure, consumers get some minimal benefit out of those programs, but just look at the information we give to companies about our spending, debt and saving patterns—all for the price of a key chain, backpack, lanyard, or a few dollars off. They are so good at it that they make us think we are winning when in truth we are just spending more and more. They know what benefits to turn on and entice us to purchase more. And, I have to say—it works!

It's a well-oiled machine that works so well that we are completely oblivious to its effects. We have become so used to its subtlety that we do not question its practices nor think about it long enough to do something about it. I wonder what would have happened if we would have objected to having our thumbprints scanned when trying to reenter the ship. Any guesses?

The difference in knowing that the Marketing Machine exists while on the Journey to financial victory is that you must become keenly aware of its influence. Every purchase you make must be thoroughly and consciously considered before the purchase is made. Frivolous spending and spending without accountability or consideration of consequences must come to an end if you plan to take this journey. Making emotional purchases is just as unhealthy as emotional eating or an unhealthy lifestyle. Justifying purchases without real need and failing to plan for the future can be just as damaging as physical or emotional abuse.

A lot of your spending habits can be traced to giving in to and buying into marketing ploys. Many times, we hear or see something that triggers an emotion or fulfills a need within us and we lose our power over purchase. It's not difficult to change your financial course, but it must be done for your family's sake and yours. Ignoring subliminal and blatant messages from the Marketing Machine is not easy. I'll be the first to admit that. They are experts at pushing the spending buttons that can render you helpless if you allow them to. But in the end, you have the final say! You have the power over your financial destiny and current financial life. What you choose to do or not do with the power you have will make all the difference in your future.

Messages from a Culture of Debt

What do you want? How much do you want? You can have it all! (for a low monthly payment). You can have it now and pay for it later. I remember watching *The Flintstones* cartoon when I was a child. It was one of my favorite shows. A particular episode I have never forgotten—nor ever will— was when Wilma and

CHARGE IT!

1234 5678 1234 5678

VAILD TILL IT'S ALL GONE!

IMA N. BONDAGE

Betty discovered the power of charge (credit) cards. They could make purchases on credit and in an instant bring home things they had not yet paid for with the promise to pay later. They bought everything they could, happily shouting "Charge It!" as they made their way from store to store, filling up shopping carts and their homes with more and more stuff. At one point they became exhausted.

I do not remember that they suffered any negative consequences from their long shopping sprees. I faintly remember Fred and Barney not happy about what the girls had done, but stealing away to charge their new bowling ball purchases. If I remember correctly the ladies were able to weasel their way

out of any long-term discontentment. What a lesson! In an instant, they changed from families who saved up and paid for things to families that signed IOUs and expected a statement of debt each month. Is this really the life you want?

In the beginning of the culture of debt most families accepted by credit card companies were affluent and probably paid the balance each month, but slowly the need to pay off during each monthly Cycle began to diminish as the culture began to demand and add more and more IOUs to their monthly outflow. While Diner's Club and a few other credit companies were in existence before then to cater to the elite, this 'take and pay' phenomenon was the beginning of our nation's cultural acceptance of the Cycle of Hopelessness we find ourselves in 40+ years later.

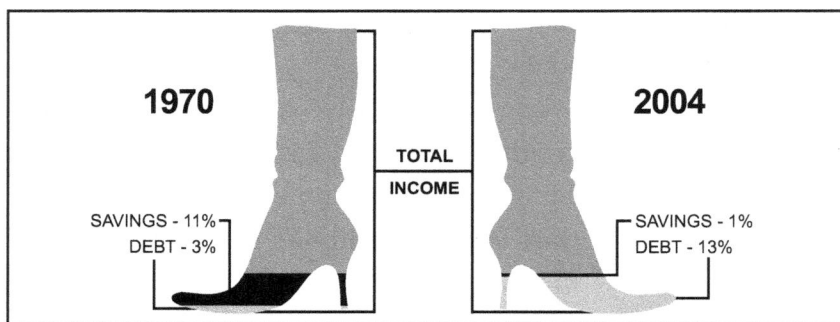

1970

2004

TOTAL
INCOME

SAVINGS - 11%
DEBT - 3%

SAVINGS - 1%
DEBT - 13%

From 1970 to 2004, according to the Federal Reserve Bank, the average household savings were 11% of income while debt payments were only three percent. Shockingly, by 2004 the average household debt payments had risen to 13 percent while savings dropped. One study found that people bought things on credit more because they wanted to have a higher standard of living than because they trusted they could repay what they borrowed. (TheCurrentMoment)

Think about it. Who was the last sales person to encourage you to make the purchase with cash? What was the last company that rewarded you for paying with cash, debit card or cashier's check? What if I told you that you do not need to build your credit as a young person, but rather build your savings? What if I told you that if you choose to "build your credit" you could do it without credit cards or a car payment?

You have probably already adjusted yourself in your seat with uneasiness by now. I will discuss those myths and how to combat them in Chapter 5. The point is that our society has created an immediate gratification culture that we have all bought into, leading to the demise of our individual and cultural financial future. We want to blame our national economy for our personal economy. Well, the truth is that if our personal economies are in order, the national economy does not matter. In fact, if our personal economy is in order we can take actions to make a positive impact on our nation and the world.

Our nation is on a path of financial destruction. I am not speaking politically. Look around you and you will find families all over hurting and even breaking up because of the pain financial stress has caused. It could be the family next door, your colleagues, relatives, or friends. With the corporate Marketing Machine watching our every move and targeting every dollar we make, we could render ourselves hopeless and give in to continuous financial woes.

You are probably reading this book because you want to find a solution to the debt, lack of savings and/or the hopelessness you feel in your life right now. You may feel that there has to be something more you can do. I'm so glad you have turned these pages. When I learned the principles and bought into the process, I became empowered—not only financially, but also within my marriage, and within myself.

Misguided Understanding and Training

There is a great lesson about financial empowerment in the animated movie *Up*. It is an excellent portrayal of a family having dreams and doing what they could to fulfill their dreams. It is a sad story, but the financial lesson in it is great. It's the story of a boy and girl who meet as kids, later fall in love, get married and begin to save for a great vacation to Paradise Island. They work and have a small savings in place. As life began to allow Murphy (that "whatever can go wrong, will go wrong" cliché) to move into their home, they need to deplete their vacation savings each time—having to start all over from zero. The story may sound familiar to you. It was a tragedy that the couple repeated this pattern over and over until they reached old age. The wife died and the husband realized they never took that vacation together. It is a sad story. The real tragedy is that they could have done something differently to reach their savings goal earlier in life, but they did not employ a different strategy for success. They could have taken different steps in securing their savings and financial future. My version of these strategies is discussed in Chapter 6.

— HOW DID WE GET THIS WAY? —

We met a couple on one of our cruises we really liked. One night at dinner on the cruise, we were talking about living in financial freedom. The couple has young adult children and like any good parents they teach their children financial lessons to prepare them for life. They desire to have their children equipped with the best toolkit life can offer and part of that toolkit is financial success. The couple began to tell us that they insisted their children take out loans and get credit cards so that they could build their credit. We shudder but remember that their intentions are pure. They want the best for their children. And so do we. Thank God we were able to share with them ways in which their children could build their own financial identity and do it without adding debt. We may never know if they entertained the financial behavior change we suggested, but they did hear about options that could change their family legacy.

Again, you are in control of your financial destiny. This is a race. It does not matter where you are when you begin, but that you begin, continue and finish the race. You will find that there are many, many rewards along the way that will sustain you until you get to your goal. Once you reach your first financial goal it sets the stage for more. Bradley and I did set goals and still do. But now we are in a very different place financially than when we began. Our lives are so much more fulfilled and full of purpose than before. The Journey to living financially victorious came at a price, but the benefit in our lives far outweighs the price we paid. We really regretted the fact that we did not know earlier in life the principles and strategies that enabled us to win financially. They are priceless for those who dare to put them to use.

Additionally, you are not on this journey alone. As a trained financial coach I have some resources for you to utilize. You may contact me for encouragement and help if you get stuck along the way.

Chapter 2 Take-Aways

List three insights you gained from this chapter.

1.

2.

3.

List three things you learned about yourself.

1.

2.

3.

List three behaviors/actions you will change and specify why.

1.

2.

3.

CHAPTER 3

What Can We Do To Fix The Problem?

Does a Problem Exist?

You've heard it before. In order to fix something you have to admit that a problem exists. Perhaps you know back in the recesses of your mind that your financial outgo significantly exceeds your income. You avoid calls from bill collectors, throw away financial statements from banks, and ignore billing statements from creditors, but continue to spend and borrow in the quest to have more stuff. You have what I call a case of Avoidance. Never in the history of mankind (I presume) has avoiding something made it go away—especially in one's finances. No, your financial distress will continue to haunt you if you try to ignore it.

Avoidance is not the answer. You would think that admitting a financial problem exists is easy. Oh, far from that! There are so many emotions tied into what you decide to do with your money. If I told you that you should cut up all of your credit cards and never use them again, you would probably have a physiological reaction, "a fit"—your blood pressure or heart rate may increase, and you go into defense mode, justifying all the reasons you need to keep at least one. Well, in my opinion you don't need any, and you should cut up them all.

I frequently hear well-known television financial gurus tell people they need to keep at least two credit cards. I vehemently disagree with this philosophy. The first reason is that it is likely that these gurus get kick-backs/profit for promoting credit card usage. One guru promotes her own prepaid MasterCard and teaches personal finance at one of the private online universities being investigated for unlawful recruiting and financial aid practices. The problem is that she teaches people to avoid high cost institutions like this if they are unaffordable.

The second reason is that I know this is not true. I paid off our last credit card in 2005. I have not used one since that time. You mean to tell me that the well-paid TV financial gurus who have it all figured out have not tried to live without credit cards? Or, perhaps they are so wealthy now that they do not use credit cards, but will tell you that you need to do so. I'm here to set the record straight. I cannot think of one reason I have needed to use a credit card for the last eight years. Not once. Not even to use it and pay it off within the allotted time. You can play this game if you like, but you are likely to lose at some point. Just see what happens if the payment doesn't make it in time or you experience a job loss and this one is not high on your "pay right now" list. The vast majority of people do not pay on time—even those who intended to do so. This is how they make billions of dollars off of consumers. Avoid cards like the plague.

The financial gurus say you need these credit cards for emergencies. I say it and Bradley and I teach our workshop participants that in order to live victoriously you build your savings account(s) to be able to catch you when life's emergencies happen, instead of holding on to debt accumulation practices that no longer work. We are not alone; Bradley and I know plenty of people (at all income levels) who ditched credit cards and debt and who are making it just fine without those crutches in their financial toolkit. You can live this way as well and in my chapter on the Financial Toolkit you will learn how easy it can be.

Behavior Change

What we are really talking about in this chapter is behavior change. The financial woes of Americans can be traced back to their behavior. That's right! Behavior! Think about the family who is on the verge of losing their home. Many times you will find that the family either financed too much house or did not have a sufficient Rainy Day savings that would take care of this number one asset in the case of income loss.

I have no judgment about families who have lost their homes—in fact, I think it is tragic—but I do know that there is a way to secure this asset. There are so many positive alternatives and options you can employ that will cushion you from life's curve balls and allow you to emerge from challenging times victoriously. Your responsibility in all of this is to make written and verbal commitments to change your behavior. Obviously your past behavior was not allowing you to win, so to admit you have a problem and be willing to make a commitment to change is huge! When you commit to change, you give the universe an opportunity to show you a new, more productive way of accomplishing something. When you commit to change, you admit that your way did not work and open yourself up to the benefits of wisdom others can provide as you take this Journey.

Profession to Others

Accountability comes in different forms. When there is a major change needed in your life, it is wise to find others who can support your effort. These people will give you the accountability you need to keep you on course and motivated to accomplish your financial goals. It's not easy to admit that change is necessary and certainly not easy to make a commitment to change; likewise, it can be difficult to put yourself out there and let others know that you have made a commitment to take a different course financially that will position you to win.

This act cannot be avoided on your journey, so be sure to profess your behavioral change to as many people as you can. You don't have to share with them the details of your financial situation, just let them know that changes will take place and the change may affect your relationship with them in a positive way. Ask for their support and they will help you win the battle. You need them and they need the lessons you will teach them.

— WHAT CAN WE DO TO FIX THE PROBLEM? —

CHAPTER 3 TAKE-AWAYS

List three areas in your life where you have identified a problem.

1.

2.

3.

List three ways in which you intend to change your life.

1.

2.

3.

List at least three people you will profess your changes to who will hold you accountable.

1.

2.

3.

4.

5.

CHAPTER 4

What Will It Take to Change?

Knowledge of Financial Condition

Similar to admitting you have a financial problem is coming to terms with your real financial condition. Your role here is to take an honest look at exactly what your assets, debts and resources are. If you fail to incorporate this step, it is impossible for you to move forward into financial freedom. It's time to look at everything on paper again or for the first time.

I remember when Bradley and I sat down to do this step. Well, maybe we didn't actually sit down together. I think I gathered everything, put it on paper, and showed it to him. It was quite shocking to see that we owed consumer debt of over $60,000 in addition to our home mortgage! Wowza! How in the world were we going to conquer that? It looked daunting and impossible. We thought we would have been just as well to forget it and just work to pay bills the rest of our lives.

But it had to be done. We had to look our financial situation square in the face. At that point we considered it a bully on the playground and neither one of us were accustomed to backing down from bullies. So we decided to stare the bully in the face and take him down head-on. Facing the financial bully helped us come to know our exact position in our war against debt.

Alternative Behavior

After we faced our financial bully we had to get ready for our new behavior in order to beat the financial distress in our lives. We had to put every old behavior and their justifications on the table. There were a few of them that we kept because they were at least leading us in the right direction (i.e. writing monthly budget on paper, keeping financial papers in order, making payments on time). Honestly, we just had to tweak them a bit so that we could maximize their effectiveness. But the rest of our behaviors were called out and put on notice. No longer could I spend each Sunday headed to the malls and stores with newspaper circulars in hand. No longer could I refuse to save for emergencies. No longer could I continue with the attitude that I deserved a new car, Dooney & Burke, Coach, cultured pearls and $1,000 pumps when I had no money in the bank to show for it. It had to stop! I had to adopt a new way of looking at who I was through God's eyes and not man's.

When you adopt this step, it won't take you long to realize that no one really cares about the car you drive, the shoes you wear or the purse you carry. It's all a façade. It's an imaginary world we dream up in our minds to help us feel good about our spending and ourselves. You will soon realize what is really important and it all begins with behavior change. So get ready to uncover some productive behaviors you don't realize you are capable of owning and exercising. You will be amazed and proud of the transformation you are about to make! It was the most wonderful transformation of my life.

Prepare Financial Toolkit for Success

Getting prepared to make such drastic behavior change is necessary as well. I'll make it easy for you. This is the time to be honest and put everything on the table. Even those items you forgot about or hoped you forgot. You may have to go way back in your financial history to retrieve some of them. Remember, if you made a debt, it is your responsibility to pay it back! There's no getting around that. It keeps you honest and helps you sleep at night. Now if you have a debt that is a "sleeping giant," for the time being, you may wish to let it continue to sleep; and then when it is time to pay it off you surprise the giant and slay it with one payment you have saved over time for this purpose.

Here is a list of things you will need to gather and have ready to begin your transformation. There may be additional items for use with your financial toolkit, but this list will at least get you started.

    a. Recent credit reports—These may contain items you may have forgotten or that you need to have removed. You can obtain a FREE report from each of the three credit bureaus each year; pull all three reports at the same time as each may have different items listed. This government endorsed website is where you can obtain your reports free each year; you may have to bypass the "purchase your credit score" options to get to the FREE reports; save on your computer and print one each from Transunion, Equifax, and Experian. www.annualcreditreport.com. With your pen in hand, make notes of any entries that are inaccurate or not yours by marriage in a community property state. You will dispute these.

b. Credit cards—list each with balances owed, minimum payment, and payment dates.

c. Auto loans—list each with balances owed, minimum payment, and payment dates.

d. Student loans—subsidized, unsubsidized, and private (whether or not you graduated or completed the certification); list each with balances owed, minimum payment, and payment dates.

e. Family/Friend IOUs—These people will be amazed (and thankful) that you are going to pay them back! You might even consider negotiating a lower payoff amount if you feel they won't be offended. First let them know of your genuine intent to pay them in the very near future.

f. Retirement accounts—gather papers and costs.

g. Life insurance—gather papers, premiums and coverage amounts.

h. Paper, pen, calculator—when used these are very effective in showing your financial reality.

i. Any other papers or accounts that have financial impact or implications.

Whew! That's it for now. It's a lot, but it'll keep you honest. I suggest you keep these items in a secured file cabinet or box so that you may easily access them any time you need them.

I know you are wondering, "how long will this take?" Well, the answer to that question is so complex that I really can't give you a straight answer. Why? There are so many variables involved. I can tell you that families and individuals I have worked with have testified about immediate results and changes in their lives. I would say it takes the average family or individual 18-24 months to become debt free.

Here are some of the variables that come into play to determine how long it might take a family/individual to dump their debt:

- Depends on amount of debt
- Depends on savings goals
- Depends on age/family size
- Depends on income
- Depends on commitment (total family, but begins with self)

Most of all it depends on your intensity and desire to do whatever it takes to make this happen. Commitment! This is the number one factor, in my opinion, to make a new financial life a reality. When Bradley and I first began our journey, we looked back after 5 years and had not made much progress.

However, when we decided to pull out all of the stops and get really intense we were able to eliminate ALL of our debt within 13 months. Yes! I want the same for you! It can happen and you can make it happen! I know you can!

Chapter 4 Take-Aways

Describe your "Aha! Moment" concerning your financial condition.

List three things you already have in your financial toolkit.

1.

2.

3.

List the three most critical things you need to add to your financial toolkit in the next week.

1.

2.

3.

CHAPTER 5

Financial Myths

There are so many myths out there about how to handle your financial life. Most of the myths are perpetuated by people who don't know any better, some by people who do know better, and some are just out there in the stratosphere for us to believe if we do not have accurate information and knowledge to discredit them. Before you get too far on this journey I think it might be helpful to dispel some of the most common financial myths that I have heard from clients and participants in our lectures and seminars.

Myth 1—I need debt to build my credit

The Credit Score

Watch television, the news, or listen to any radio station for long and you will come to believe that your credit score is the number one ticket to having the status you want in life. You hear of companies that can tell you what your credit score is and some that can help you get a higher score. The goal is to have the highest score possible and if you don't it implies that you are somehow deficient as a person. The connotation also implies that only "good people" have high credit scores of over 760.

You've also learned that without a good credit score, you can't get a good job, can't get good insurance, and can't get a good interest rate for your home, car or other purchases. In my opinion this is probably the biggest myth in our society. And we teach our children all the tenets of this myth as though it were true.

If you utilize the process outlined in this book, everything you purchase will be self-financed, so competitive interest rates will no longer apply to you. Discounts you may have received on insurance premiums will not outweigh your "pay cash in advance" discount and your credit report may have a low score, but you will be free of creditors. I have not financed anything in six years and our credit scores remain above 790. It may take a decade or longer for our scores to plummet, but even then it will not matter.

I'll Spend More on Insurance!

My curiosity had me fact-check the effects of a "good" credit score on insurance. I phoned several insurance companies and polled some HR executives I know. The insurance companies understand that "low credit score" rates happen to good people as well. For example, it is common for an elderly couple to have paid their mortgage and owe little to no debt. The insurance algorithms cause this couple's rates to be a little higher than those of another couple with debt and a higher credit score. But when you think about it, the proof is in the mathematics. The couple with no debt pays a slightly higher insurance premium, but pays no interest to creditors, while the couple with debt gets a small insurance premium discount, but pays hundreds or thousands of dollars in interest to creditors each year. Who gets the better deal?

I Can't Get Hired Without Good A Credit Score

As for future employers, they are not looking at the score, per se, but rather your financial behavior. They are more interested in your financial behavior than a score. They judge from your financial behavior whether you are trustworthy and dependable. According to a recent article from CBS Money Watch, "The use of credit reports is particularly common with people hired for positions with financial responsibilities or handling sensitive employee information." This segment of workers is only a fraction of the workforce, which means this is not applicable to the vast majority of employees.

My most recent employer did not conduct a credit check, but they did conduct a criminal background check as they do with all employees. Your future employers may or may not reference your credit report, but before that happens there are many things you can do to make sure you are seen in the best light regardless of your credit score without going into debt (or adding debt).

It's Your Debt So Pay It Back!

Let me be clear. If you owe a debt, you are obligated to pay it. Period. It is your responsibility to honor your commitment to make at least the minimum payments on your debts and to do it in a timely manner. It's part of being a good, responsible citizen. And when that cannot happen, you should be in communication with your creditors about your situation.

It is also important to make sure your credit reports are accurate and up-to-date. You do not need to pay someone else to repair your credit. You can do it yourself. Mark your calendar each year to download your credit report. Do this on your birthday or anniversary, but do it every year. You can get it for free at www.annualcreditreport.com. Get one from each of the three reporting bureaus. This is a great way to keep an eye on your financial activity and check for errors. Be sure to dispute any errors you find immediately. If you have a special situation on your report that you need to explain to a prospective employer, I recommend that you do so verbally and in writing after you accept the job offer so that when your credit report is evaluated they will not be surprised. It may or may not affect their decision, but you can have peace knowing you exercised due diligence. Sometimes not knowing in advance causes employers to believe that you were trying to be deceptive.

Alternatives to Buying Debt to Build Credit

If you are like I was, you teach your children that they have to build their credit so that they "look good" for those people watching their credit report. Any good parent would do this with the best intentions. So you get them their first credit card, auto loan, signature loan and co-sign for them with hopes that they will make good on their debt. It's really a bad idea and there are alternatives that will yield the same or a similar outcome.

One way is to build positive financial behavior is to pay your bills on time. Along this Journey you will be forced to decide how much to pay to which creditor. We will always recommend making the minimum monthly payment and then decide which creditor will get more. We will discuss this in greater detail in the next chapter.

Morally and legally, paying your bills on time shows positive financial behavior and it will show up for whoever is looking for it. You avoid fees, phone calls and headaches by making regular payments on the debts you owe. You also set a great example of honoring your commitment to those around you.

Keeping a good job is important in so many ways, but it can also prove that you have good intentions financially. It is my third suggestion for building positive financial behaviors without going into more.

Myth 2—Husbands, Wives and Bank Accounts

I hear from women everywhere about their bank accounts that are separate from their husband's bank accounts. More commonly I hear about the "secret" account that Mama told them to have to hide money from their husbands. Well dear, there are all kinds of moral, spiritual, personal, and marital issues with regard to this recommendation.

From the month Bradley and I were wed, we joined bank accounts. All of them. We learned about *The Salt Covenant* that existed in ancient times. In this covenant, business would be conducted and solidified when each party poured some of the salt from his pouch into the pouch of the other party. If one wanted to back out of the agreement he had to go into the other pouch and find his salt. Impossible, right?

So is the covenant of marriage. "Two shall become one." Remember that? It is true in all matters of marriage. I see no need to hide money from my husband. I trust him and what we have together in this marriage we built together, so we have no need to separate anything. We are a team! I honor him and he honors me.

I understand that there may be circumstances when separate accounts are necessary such as in the cases of addiction or abuse. If this is your situation, you need to do what is necessary to protect yourself, your children, and your home. What I am really talking about are cases where issues from childhood, selfishness, and mistrust in each other are at the root of having separate accounts. Those are marital, emotional and/or psychological issues, not financial issues, and they may require professional help in that regard.

Myth 3—If I Had A Higher Paying Job My Financial Situation Would Be Better

Not really. In fact, participants in our workshops, classes and lectures have come from all walks of life and income levels. We have found that one's income level does not determine financial behavior; only behavior does. We discussed in earlier chapters that the American way is living above our income level. This has to be reversed. We have had low-income students who made a conscious decision to live within their income level and win financially. No, they probably won't have the lifestyle of the rich and famous, but they have a lifestyle they are comfortable with. If you live below your means you can have this financial peace too. The problem is that most Americans want what is seen on television or at the house next door.

The only thing to do about your income level if you think it's too low is to raise it. You've got to earn more and/or do something on the side that will guarantee you more income. We learned in one of our trainings that "your income is your greatest wealth building tool" (Dave Ramsey). Whatever you have to do to earn more money, do it as long as it is legal, moral and ethical! I suggest staying away from pyramid or multi-level marketing income generators. Research shows that the vast majority of people involved in these schemes lose money over the life of their involvement instead of earning money. However, the choice is always yours.

Instead, think of what you can do with your hands, head, or feet, or from your heart. For example, some women are great at fashion. I would pay someone to come into my closet, organize it, and show me new ways to wear the clothing I already have. I love shopping in my own closet! I just don't have time to optimize what is already there. Perhaps you can help organize someone's home office, cook, clean, tutor math, teach sports, give piano lessons, give voice lessons or serve as a virtual assistant. Think of just about anything you are gifted at and willing to do for someone that can earn you money on a regular basis. You don't have to open a business if you don't want to; just earn some money so that you can build wealth.

Another alternative to raising your income level is to sell some stuff. Sell everything that is not bolted down. Really. Take a look around the rooms in your house. When did we become a society of hoarders? I don't mean like the people on television. I mean you are just collecting and keeping stuff because...it's sentimental, it was a gift, you might use it one day, it'll be useful when you ____. Do you get what I mean now? Start stacking up so much stuff by the garage and the dog thinks he's going too. There are many ways to earn money from the stuff you have right in your home instead of giving it to Goodwill, but save a stack for charity as well.

This summer is going to be a major "purge the closets, garage and deck" event for the Vinson family. I'll post on the blog how much we earned when we sold stuff. I recommend you do this once every two years or more often if you can.

Myth 4—My Children Deserve a Better Life Than I Had

I love this one. It's not really a myth as much as it is an excuse to justify bad financial behaviors. It may be true that your children deserve a better life than you had. The question becomes 'to what extent?' I have two children in their twenties and I am currently raising my two young grandchildren. I love them and want the best for the four of them. I have learned, though, to have limits on what I will do for them.

First let me say that in raising children we (parents, guardians, care givers) are required to provide reasonable food, shelter, clothing and transportation. The qualifier is "reasonable" and I believe this is where we get it all twisted. Just because you didn't get the Nike shoes when all the other kids had them does not mean your children need a closet full of Nike shoes, clothes, cell phones, eating out, and other luxuries you cannot afford. If you follow the plan outlined in the book, there will be a time when getting them the luxuries of life will be worthwhile and meaningful and make sense to your family.

I'm not sure where mothers allow this imaginary guilt trip to get the best of them. Your children will be ok with less stuff. Believe me, I know how you feel. Something hurts deep on the inside when we have to tell our children "No!" We regret it—convincing ourselves if we don't give them everything they ask for they will be damaged somehow. But the best lesson you can teach your children is how to be responsible with money so that they can maintain good financial behavior throughout their lives. You really want them to learn how to win now because they will then be good stewards of the legacy you leave behind. Teaching them good money habits now will ensure that the legacy you leave them will be valued and cared for and not spent frivolously. The investment you make now in their learning fiscal responsibility will allow your children to live richer lives. The alternative is to continue to provide them with lots of stuff now and not have a legacy to leave them later.

One day I looked in my teenage daughter's closet and realized she had more clothes and shoes than I did and she wore very few of them. What was I teaching her about her value and worth? What if rather than giving her everything, she earned what she desired? I did that after I had the closet encounter. Funny thing was that when she had to work (around the house, special errands, job, etc.) for her stuff, she put the brakes on spending and everything began to have value. She even put herself through Barbizon Modeling School. She threw a few teentrums, but after a while she matured and was grateful for the lesson. In her twenties now, she's very aware of where her money goes and the purposes it serves. I'm very proud of her accomplishments and I know that part of her financial success will be because of the positive financial lessons I taught her.

You know that your son or daughter will be involved in soccer or baseball next year and you know the expense involved with that. How about having the child earn the money to cover the cost of the activity they want to be involved in. Alone or with your help in long-term planning for these expenses, your household budget does not take a hit when the surprise registration comes up every year in September. You can do this with anything you know or have a hunch will happen. Prom is a great example. So are school pictures, field trips, and fundraisers. Live a "no surprises" life when it comes to the kids.

Be careful about the messages you listen to and tell yourself when it comes to your children. You will be surprised how little they require of you financially. You know the stories of those of us who grew up in poverty but didn't realize we were poor. That's because the love in our households was so strong that it shielded us from societal norms. Your love is the biggest gift you can give your children. Trust that when you give them what the family can afford at the time, it is enough. It is possible that your children will not get to participate in everything other children do. It is possible they won't have the latest this or that while you climb your way out of debt. But remember that it is only for a season. You will learn to do very special things that are low cost or free that will provide long-lasting memories for them. When you claim financial victory you will be in a better position to go get some more stuff and do some more things, but for now you will want to establish limits. So do not allow feelings of guilt to dictate what you should or should not do for your children. Devise a plan with their input and follow it.

CHAPTER 5 TAKE-AWAYS

List three financial myths you believed.

1.

2.

3.

List three things you learned about yourself.

1.

2.

3.

List three behaviors you will change and say why.

1.

2.

3.

CHAPTER 6

Taking Control: Your Financial Toolkit

The PROCESS

Remember the list of items I suggested you gather, in Chapter 4? Well, it's time to get them and put them to good use. In this chapter, we will discuss the time-tested, proven method that will get you on a direct course to win financially. To win is a relative term and may have different meanings for different people. In my view, when you win financially you have eliminated debt, have a firm savings in place, and are building wealth that will change your family tree.

What Does it Mean to
WIN,
Financially?

The process you will learn in this lesson is not new. It's actually rather old, and commonly used. A generation or two ago people used to live by these methods instead of the debtors' lifestyle that is so popular in America today. I did not create any of the steps; in fact I have borrowed them from sources I have come across in my own debt-free journey and since then. The process is not easy to walk through and you may have trouble at a place or two.

I recommend that you have a person to walk beside you on this journey (your spouse if you are married). As I mentioned in a previous chapter, this financial freedom partner must be someone you trust, can share financial information with (to whatever extent you feel comfortable), and can speak truth to you if he or she sees you are about to make a bad financial decision. This person is not your shopping buddy or someone who has a bleak outlook on life. This person will cheer you to victory as you cross the financial freedom finish line.

Here are the steps in the process as Bradley and I teach them in our seminars and keynote speeches to groups, couples, men and women:

1. Hope

Bradley and I were called by God to do this work in April 2012— exactly 5 years from when we became free from the bondage of debt. Our first mission is to provide hope to you and others like you so that you can believe you no longer have to live under the bondage of debt. It may be a long Journey to debt freedom, but you can make it. It is against the laws of nature and God for you to be in financial bondage.

In his book, *Men, Get Real With Your Finances...It Takes More Than Money to Win*, Bradley discovered more passages related to financial matters than any other subject in the

Bible. Two particular scriptures summarize what God's word intended for us to do financially. The book of Proverbs (22:7) teaches that debt is equivalent to financial bondage. And, Romans 13:8 reminds us that we are not meant to be indebted to anyone, but to have freedom in life to love others. When we are free from financial bondage, we have the freedom to love and share our lives with others in a totally different way. My message begins with hope—for you, your family, your community, our nation, and our world.

2. The Four Foundational Walls

You may be in a place financially where creditors are sending you threatening mail or harassing you on the phone to collect the money you owe them. Although they have the right (within the limits of the law) to communicate with you to collect debt, they too have developed techniques similar to the Marketing Machine that will cause you to have a serious enough emotional response (i.e. shame, anger, embarrassment) that you will not only give them their money instead of paying your electric bill or paying your rent/mortgage, but you will give them full access to your banking accounts. Yes, you are obligated to return money you signed a note for, but you get to decide when and how that is done. And, never, ever give a debt collector access to your accounts—they will drain them leaving you nothing but a burden to try to get money back.

The safety and security of your home life is very important! I want you to first take care of your Four Foundational Walls as a life priority. The Four Foundational Walls provide you the protection you and your family need. You will build fortification around the things you have to protect from creditors and life's other events.

Assuming you have reasonable transportation, shelter, food and clothing allotments, your stability and peace of mind will come in having this foundation in place. I say reasonable because a cash car, eating at home instead of restaurants, whatever untattered clothes you can get your hands on for now, and shelter that is no more than 25% of your household take-home pay is what I consider reasonable; anything above that for now is unreasonable and unnecessary while you are climbing out of debt. Here is the make up of the Four Foundational Walls:

Food—you set a reasonable amount aside each paycheck to cover your eating at home for dinner and on weekends. Do not pay creditors from this allotment. You must eat to win, but you don't have to eat extravagantly. When I lived in New Orleans for a few years I learned to love red beans and rice on Mondays, which traditionally was laundry day. No time to cook, so dinner consisted of this culinary delight. You will have to live on simple, but nutritious food like this while you get out of debt. It sure isn't Saltgrass Steakhouse or Your Favorite Grill, but those places won't pay your debt off either. It's time to start making tough but smart choices about where your money goes.

Shelter—this includes utilities. If your rent/mortgage is more than 25% of your take home pay you have too much shelter right now. Consider moving to a more affordable domain. Also, look for ways to cut your utilities by comparing service providers. By the way, cable TV is not a utility; it is a luxury. The $100-$200 per month you send to the cable company can be put to better use to eliminate debt. The same is true with your cell phone and telephone. Rethink the true purposes for your paying for these each month. You need to cut these expenses down or out. What are you willing to do to win financially?

Clothing—the good thing about clothing is that it mostly lasts a very long time. I believe that you see the importance of cutting expenses. Your clothing is sufficient. You do not need the latest, hottest fashion to make it in life or to be liked. You need clothing for work and some for play. Whatever you have right now should last you for at least a year. The children will grow. I know this is a shock, but they will grow. You will be able to plan ahead for their clothing needs. But, chances are your wardrobe will not need to be updated for years. In fact, you may want to write a shopping spree into your budget after your debt is paid to update your wardrobe. In the meantime, if you can agree that you will look just fine and no one really cares what you wear while you get out of debt, you can win much sooner. Put off shopping for clothing items unless ab- solutely necessary. When you go, take a very specific list of things to buy with a budget and purchase nothing else. Re- member, the stores will have sales when you get out of debt.

Transportation—reliable transportation—is critical. I do not suggest that you own or keep high interest, high payment or leased vehicles. If you have such a vehicle or are upside down on your loan, unload it. Great reliable cash cars that do not add a burden on your family are for sale everywhere. Depending on where you live, public transportation is a great option as well.

Rainy Day Fund (RDF)—This is the fictitious character called Murphy. The adage says, "whatever can go wrong, will go wrong." This is Murphy's motto. The full Rainy Day Fund will act as the covering for your Four Foundational Walls and Murphy-repellant. I will discuss how this works in Step 5, but when it is in place you can relax your mind and concentrate fully on the process without living in fear of what you will do when something goes wrong.

3. Granny's Purse

I remember that when I was a child my grandmother had money in a small change purse she hid in her bosom. She had a lot of dollar bills crumpled up in that change purse and every now and then she would slip one to me. I quickly ran to the corner store for sweet treats. She would always say to me that I needed to put some money back for emergencies. I also found out that my grandmother had a larger purse under her mattress. In that purse she kept hundreds of dollars in cash. She was not a fan of taking money to the bank (given her experiences during the Great Depression I suppose), so she kept her savings quietly hidden under her mattress.

The lesson I learned from her is the importance of putting aside money for small emergencies and for larger unplanned events. When Granny (as I affectionately called her) would need to have repairs around the house or with that car, she would go into her purse for the money to take care of whatever was wrong. She didn't balk about it, cry about it, or feel stress. That's what the set-aside money was for.

As soon as you begin your Journey, the washer will break, tires go flat, AC needs repairing, kids need tooth fillings or some other nuisance event will happen to destroy your effort. This acts as a "mini" Rainy Day Fund (RDF) and will catch your slack so that you don't go to credit cards or payday loans.

It is so important to have emergency savings as you make your way on this journey. If your household income is below $20,000 I recommend you set aside at least $500 for life's emergencies. If your household income is $20,000 or greater I recommend at least $1,000. This is cash money you can get your hands on quickly. You may not like the idea of having that much cash under your mattress. That's okay. Take it down to the local bank, lock box or wherever makes you comfortable. This is just a plain savings account. It is not meant to be an investment account. This small amount needs to be accessible without penalty so that you can get your emergency taken care of quickly. And, you will have to make a vow not to touch it except for a bon-a-fide emergency that you and your financial partner have agreed is worthy.

When Bradley and I saved our $1,000 we quickly realized that I was not comfortable with only that amount. Since my family lived so far away, if we needed to get to them for a family emergency, we would need airfare...for four people. So we eventually doubled, then tripled the amount in our Granny's

Purse account until I was finally at peace. I knew that whatever came up, we were prepared financially to handle it.

It is very important to get this cash in the bank quickly. I want you to set a 30-day goal for this. **As you find extra cash from your income, do not run and try to pay something off. Add it to your Granny's Purse account.** Why? If you delay getting this in place, things in your life will start to break down and need repair. If you've dedicated the spare cash to paying something off early you will need to add more debt to get the repair done instead of taking it from Granny's Purse —compounding the problem.

I know you are asking where this cash will come from. We discussed earlier how you could get cash by selling stuff you have around the house. You can create other revenue streams. The question I have for you is this: if you had a deadline to have this amount to save a loved one what would you do to get the cash if you could not borrow it? Whatever you would do in this scenario, do it to get Granny's Purse in place now. When you get this fund in place you will be able to rest at night and focus on the task at hand—eliminating debt and building wealth without life's emergencies causing you to go back into debt. Remember, you have 30 days to complete this task. This is the covering or roof for your Four Foundational Walls. Trust me, when it is there you will be empowered and relieved. GO!

4. Debt Avalanche

The next phase in this process after you have your Granny's Purse fund in place is to attack your debt as though it's a bad habit. Signing up for debt is a bad habit our entire nation has adopted, but it's time to establish new, healthy financial behavior that will put you in a better position to win with money. There is an easy plan to eliminate debt. Following the steps below is the easiest, fastest method. This method will provide you with small victories along the way to keep you motivated and see the results of your efforts quickly.

Debt Avalanche Form

Item	Total Payoff	Minimum Payment	New Payment
Macy's	$100	$15	(yard sale)
Home Depot	$430	$15	$30
Signature Loan	$550	$70	$100
Discover	$1,200	$100	$200
Car	$4,000	$150	$350
Student Loan	$8,000	$110	$460

a. List your consumer debt from smallest balance to largest balance (ignore interest rates here). Do not add your mortgage debt to this list. You will attack the mortgage at a later time in the process.

b. Find unclaimed money in your budget, yard sale, etc., to add to debt elimination.

c. Pay minimum amount due on each debt.

d. Add the extra money you found in your budget to the minimum of the first (lowest balance) debt until it is paid.

e. Add the extra money and the amount you paid on the first debt to the second debt until it is paid.

f. Keep finding extra money and adding everything you paid on the previous debt to the next.

You have now triggered a debt avalanche. Once your avalanche begins to descend, do not let it stop until it smothers all the debt in its pathway. It takes the average family 18-24 months to eliminate all of the consumer debt they created before engaging in this process. Depending on your income, debt and other variables, it may take you less or more time.

5. Rainy Day Fund (RDF)

After your debt avalanche has destroyed your consumer debt you will feel so free that you probably will not know what to do with your money. You have been so used to sending your money to creditors that you may not know how to handle it with no one on the list to send it to. Proceed with caution.

The next place to direct your money is to deposit it in your *Rainy Day Fund*. If you have not experienced an involuntary job loss yet, chances are that you will. Or you might encounter medical needs costing more than what your insurance will allow. Or you may have unforeseen legal obligations or needs. At any rate, you should be prepared to have 6-12 months of living expenses in the bank. This is the equivalent of a very large Granny's Purse, and essentially this is the same concept, just bigger. If you lose or quit your job, this fund will carry you while you seek another job, which could easily take 6-12 months in today's economy.

What would life be like if you had no debt (except the mortgage) and had enough money in the bank to pay living expenses for up to a year? Could you relax and let life's purpose speak to you while you conduct a job search? Could you conduct a job search in a different way when you are not desperate to have money to put food on the table?

At this stage in the process, I want you to dump every dollar you can squeeze out of your budget into your Rainy Day Fund. Again, I recommend that this is in a place you can easily withdraw funds as you need them without penalty like a Money Market savings account. This type of account will earn you a little interest, but is usually not strapped with penalties that CDs and other accounts may have. Think "easy in, easy out" for your RDF.

6. Retirement, the Mortgage, and College

Now that you have your quickly accessible Granny's Purse, your debt smothered by an avalanche, and your Rainy Day Fund in place, you can concentrate your efforts on funding your retirement, eliminating mortgage debt and funding college. Depending on many variables, you will divide your discretionary income into these three important needs.

Retirement—If you unplugged your retirement contributions during your debt avalanche and RDF (highly recommended), this is the place you will want to plug back in and continue the contributions. At this point you should fund your retirement accounts to the maximum your employer will match. After your mortgage is paid in full you can make maximum deposits into your retirement with the cash that was going toward your mortgage, but for now, I recommend that you just contribute up to the amount of your employer match or 7%-10% of your income, maximum.

Mortgage pay-off—In the process, I put this step off until now for several reasons. It's probably the largest debt you have. I did not want you to put your RDF and retirement off while you attack your mortgage because it could take years. Now that you have nothing else to do with your income, I want you to save thousands of dollars in interest by paying this off as soon as you can.

Bradley and I made paying off our mortgage the number one priority after we dumped our debt and set up our retirement contributions. It is so important to dump all the debt so that your life and income is finally free to accomplish the things you need to accomplish. Imagine having hundreds or thousands of dollars free and clear each month. What could you do? Anything you want! Wouldn't it be easier to fund college, go on a vacation, support your favorite charity and enjoy so much more that life has to offer?

College funding—This is a good place in your process to make contributions to your children's college fund. Remember that college is still a luxury and is not a requirement. As long as you have a mortgage you still are in debt (technically). Your first obligation with your discretionary income is to take care of your own future in the form of having a retirement income invested and your home paid for. With that said, any contribution to the college fund you can make will be helpful. If you can't fully fund college, it is okay. Do what you can. There are plenty of debt-free options for funding college. As a college administrator I know for sure there is free money available to fund college, jobs that pay for college and work your child can do to pay for or offset college expenses.

7. *Legacy Planning*

Over the last several years I have attended many funerals and memorial services held at our church. Many families do not have the funds to even bury their departed loved one, so they resort to other, less desirable final arrangements or ask the Church and its congregation for a hand out. This is a tragedy! Not only do families not have funding for final arrangements many families are not left with a Last Will and Testament of the departed. For as little as $100 (in some cases), those you leave behind will know your wishes. **You must get a will!**

Be as specific as you can in your will. It will eliminate a lot of confusion. Here are some questions you will need to give some thought before you get the document drawn up:

> **1.** Who will care for your minor children and handle any monetary benefit they receive? Is their benefit to be used for their living expenses, education, and childcare or is it at the discretion of the caregiver?
> **2.** What about your valued or sentimental possessions or heirlooms? Do you want your possessions sold or given away? To whom? By whom?

3. Do not assume that beneficiaries of your home will know what to do with it once you are gone. Spell out who you want to live in it in the will. Or do you want them to sell it and divide the proceeds? If so, within what timeframe? Or do you want one or more beneficiaries to pay the mortgage or purchase the home? Who is responsible for the property taxes?

4. What if your first beneficiary dies in a short period after you (or at the same time)? Who is next on your list? One person or several?

5. What if the first executor you name passes away after you draw up the Will? Who will you want to oversee your wishes are carried out? If you choose a close relative, will s/he have enough clarity of mind to carry out your wishes or will they be so emotionally tied to your loss that it affects their judgment?

If one person is the primary or first beneficiary this is easier to execute, but if you name multiple beneficiaries, confusion is likely to ensue because they each may have understood your wishes with different interpretations. This is why it is so important to be as specific as possible in your will.

It is also very important in your life insurance policies to designate which beneficiary should pay for your final arrangements unless you have money set aside for this purpose separate from your policy. You may have done well by having appropriate insurance policies, and designated beneficiaries, but they do not know how the funeral will be paid. Just make it plain where the money should come from, how much and who is responsible.

In her book *If I Should Die Before I Wake: Life Celebration Planner*, my good friend and author Gail Washington has painstakingly taken the time to lay out all the necessary documents, forms, resources and processes each of us should have on hand and ready for our departure from this life. Gail's book is more like a workbook or working document that each person uses to inform family, friends, and others about their desires for their possessions, and bank, social media, insurance and other accounts. It is a great resource that I recommend everyone in your family get and work through. This will make things easier for your loved ones once you have passed away or become incapacitated.

Inheritances

I think the book of Proverbs is so applicable to people from all walks of life. In terms of legacy planning, Proverbs 13:22 says, "Good people leave an inheritance to their grandchildren...." The process I discussed in this chapter is designed to help you break free from the bondage of debt, build wealth, live victoriously and leave a proper legacy. If you follow the process you will be on a path to do just that. You can change your family tree and the social outlook for future generations.

The KEY: A Monthly Budget

The key to managing the process successfully begins with a monthly budget. You probably were hoping I completed the book without mention of this, but you are not likely to win unless you master this very important tool. It will ground you, keep you on track, show you areas that need attention, reveal your victories, and so much more! The monthly budget shows you truth about your spending habits, keeps you honest, and does not let you down.

Most people think of a monthly budget as something that will restrict them, but it is your friend and part of a two-way relationship. It's up to you to deliver the truth about where your money goes, but your budget will give you freedom to allow it to do what you want. The first few months of this process will be cumbersome and you may not get it right for a while. That's okay. My family experienced the same thing.

In fact, Bradley wanted nothing to do with the budget, but I learned to ask for 15 minutes of his time per month to "look at" the budget I had drawn up. That's what we did. The beginning of the last week of each month, I sat down with our income and expenses for the following month and put it on paper. We were taking the power over our money back by telling it what to do. I developed what is called a "zero-based budget" each month. On paper I spent every dollar we would receive the next month before the month began.

Zero-Based Budget

Budgeted Item	Sub Total	TOTAL	Actually Spent	% of Take Home Pay
CHARITABLE GIFTS		$360	_____	_____
SAVINGS				
Emergency Fund	$220		_____	
College Fund	_____	$220	_____	_____
HOUSING				
First Mortgage	$900		_____	
UTILITIES		$900		
Electricity	$200			
*FOOD			_____	
*Grocery	$250			

After our Granny's Purse Fund, all extra money went on our debt avalanche I gave it to Bradley at our monthly budget meeting for him to look over, edit, suggest, or approve. I made changes. We agreed (instead of arguing) each month about how our money would be spent the following month. Yes, we had several trial-and-error months, but after that it was smooth sailing. It took about 30 minutes in all each month once we had the rhythm and flow to the process. We have sample budget forms on our web site you can download for free. Visit www.ypeconomy.com.

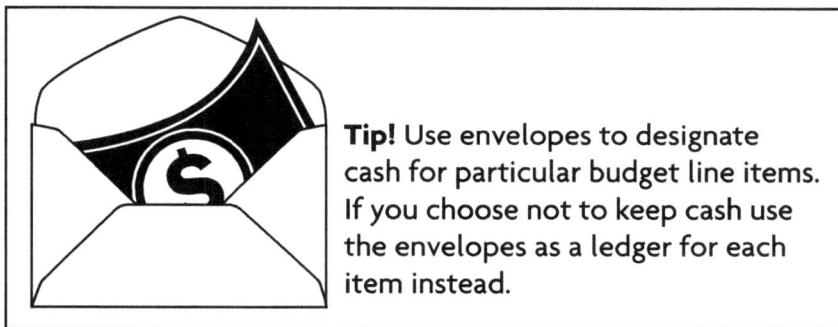

Tip! Use envelopes to designate cash for particular budget line items. If you choose not to keep cash use the envelopes as a ledger for each item instead.

In case after case, we know from others that if you skip this important step you will not win financially. Your money has to be told what to do and you have to have this discipline. It will make the other areas of the process flow so much more smoothly.

Chapter 6 Take-Aways

List three insights you gained about the process.

1.

2.

3.

List three reactions you had while reviewing the process.

1.

2.

3.

List three to five people you would like to carry out the instructions in you Last Will and Testament (Will) and your Living Will (medical instructions). This will prepare you for getting the document(s) completed quickly.

1.

2.

3.

CHAPTER 7

Emerging and Living Victoriously!

My Financial Testimony

In 1999, just a year after we were married, Bradley and I had come to the realization that while we were living the American dream, and we were drowning in debt. We sought out help through our church where the head of the finance ministry just happened to be a financial advisor. Through his company we were given a financial analysis, which revealed that along with the $60,000+ we had in consumer debt (not including our mortgage), we could expect to be debt free by the year 2012, and by 2028 including our home, "assuming the same income and no new debt." What? Thirteen years of living tightly? It sounded so ridiculously unattainable!

He sold us insurance policies and set us up with investments and other financial products. But that was it. We had no direction, no motivation, and no drive to get out of debt with such a bleak outlook. We had no idea we had $60k debt. And the mortgage too! Though he has many gifts and talents, Bradley was not gifted at budgeting and keeping up with household finances and I like crunching numbers, so it naturally fell on my plate.

In 2003 I began listening to a financial expert on a Christian radio show. What he said made sense and I kept listening once a week for at least a year or two as I drove to my doctoral classes. This guy made sense. I would go home and tell Bradley about the guy on the radio and I would implement a thing or two he suggested. But we seemed to be spinning our financial wheels, and not making any traction.

I distinctly remember praying to God to help us manage our finances better. I was doing the best I could, but there had to be a more effective way. In April 2006 a college student was in my office on the campus and I mentioned taking financial classes. She quickly responded that her mother was in charge of the classes at her church. It was the same classes suggested by the guy on the radio! I inquired and signed Bradley and myself up to start the classes in May. To my dismay, Bradley was not at all interested in attending classes on a subject he didn't really want to interact with at home. He huffed and he puffed, but we made it to the first class.

Attending the course changed our marriage. We began interacting about our financial behavior—individually and collectively. We began making changes to our behavior. In June of the following year, we celebrated complete freedom from debt, including the home mortgage! Halleluiah! We still praise God for that day and for giving us the fortitude and intensity to follow a plan and stick with it!

It was a long time from 1999 to 2007, but something happened to us in that last year. We underwent an intense (and accidental) transformation. We made up in our minds that we would change our behavior and eliminate the debt in our lives so that we could live in peace, not bondage. That same year was the first year we took a real vacation cruise. It was wonderful to celebrate the change in our lives and the victory from bondage God allowed us to know.

Effects of Lay Off

In 2012, after five years serving as a director for a university, my position (and many others) was phased out due to downsizing and budget cuts. It was emotionally devastating to know I did everything that was asked of me (and more), but still lost a job I really enjoyed. This is a real experience of many people in our country, but how many are prepared financially to weather an undetermined amount of time without steady income?

We were prepared and not pompously so. We were mostly thankful to God that we had saved for this and were prepared to enact our Rainy Day Fund. Because of this I was able to relax instead of feeling stress. I was able to apply for other jobs, release my entrepreneurial spirit, open a travel agency, and take in our grandchildren in their time of need. God is so good that none of this took a toll on our financial outcome. We even went on three cruises while I was unemployed. Most importantly, out of the job loss came the foundation of what God called me to do in support of Bradley and my mission to free people from the bondage of debt and this book!

I am thankful that after exactly one year I have started at a new place of employment in my area of expertise. I can enjoy all that the position has to offer just like in my previous position and have no financial worries on my mind. It is such a freeing and peaceful place to be.

Marital Bliss

Even now and at any point along my Journey I could have had luxury purses, strands of pearls and the most expensive pumps. Before the process, Bradley and I were on the verge of throwing in the towel on our marriage. Like many couples, we used our bad financial behavior as an excuse for what was wrong with our marriage. It took lots of prayer and time to heal us, but I know in my heart that if we had not changed our bad financial behavior, we would not have made it this far.

The stuff we acquire is just stuff. I could have had a lot of it back then and now. Instead, I like what I have—a peaceful home life, and a husband who loves God and me. Because of this process, my marriage has been strengthened when it used to be strained. My access to people, places and things has increased. My relationship with God is off the charts and I have peace, patience and a positive future.

Victorious Living

In order to live victoriously as we have described in this chapter (and perhaps that looks a little differently for you) requires discipline, commitment and sacrifice. It takes all three areas and consistency in all three to live a life that is free from the bondage of debt, prepared for life's curve balls, and ready to serve others. You see, we can collect all the stuff the world has to offer, but if it has no meaning it has no worth.

Think of someone you know who has closets full of clothes and shoes. My friends consistently tell me about their stuff, "I don't need all this, but...." What if they had taken the value of what is in their closets and paid off their mortgage or car, or saved for college? I'm not saying we don't need or deserve nice things, but I am calling into question what value we place on these things. I'm calling into question whether we choose to continue the behavior that got us into our messes in the first place. I'm calling into question the very fiber of our being that causes us to misbehave. And I'm calling it out so that you will do better. Dr. Maya Angelou said, "When we know better, we do better." My friend, you must do better!

Bradley talks about *opportunity-cost* in his keynote speeches and seminars. It means that every dollar we earn can only be spent once. We get to decide if it is used for stuff or savings, for college fund or eating out every day, for retirement savings or car payments. Whatever you choose to do with it, you only have one shot at it.

Now that you have worked the process to this point, it is time for you to live, live, live! Go ahead and get yourself some *Purses, Pearls and Pumps*, but vow to never let them get you. When we came to the stage of the process where we were debt-free, I could not just go buy a bunch of stuff! Every dollar I spend now has to have a specific purpose and meaning. I don't purchase things to please others any more. If I buy shoes, it is time for shoes. If I purchase jewelry it is usually costume jewelry; if they are high dollar items, I have won them at auctions or saved up and paid cash for. I still recommend that you have a budget for your purchases so that you don't go overboard.

You are also in a position to give, give, and give! Not only for tax return purposes, but you will find that the more you give to others of your time or resources, the more fulfilling your life will be. You may have said that you always wanted to support your church or a charity in a significant way. Now is the time to make a commitment. Now that you have changed your destiny and legacy, you can also change the destiny of others.

Whose Money Is It Anyway?
Whether you are Christian or not, if you get this one thing your entire life will have a new perspective. The money really isn't yours. Think about it. You are a steward of the money that passes through your hands. You may have earned it or someone may have given it to you, but it can be gone just as easily as it has come to you.

The earth is the Lord's and everything in it! (Psalm 24:1) You can't take anything with you into the next life. God calls for you to manage your resources with great integrity. Recently, we announced our calling to take this message, this ministry to our community, so that people might learn how they can become free from the burden of debt and go on to live victorious lives. We have never experienced random people literally giving money to this ministry. We have been given financial gifts that we did not ask for and we will use them wisely and with integrity to further this work! It's awesome to see God honor our stewardship and commitment to Him. I know that my personal relationship with Christ Jesus has been the glue that has held everything in my life together while I worked through this process from end to end. He guides me and gives me wisdom that makes me a good steward of the resources He has entrusted to me. And guess what? He can do the same for you!

Chapter 7 Take-Aways

List three insights you gained from this chapter.

1.

2.

3.

What is the "stuff" you will have to come to terms with? List three of those here.

1.

2.

3.

List three behaviors you will change and state why.

1.

2.

3.

Chapter 8

A Few Final Thoughts

The words and concepts in this book are my own (unless otherwise noted) based on my experiences, readings, trainings, and certification. I am not a therapist, accountant, tax or other attorney, financial planner or advisor. I have a doctorate degree with expertise in college administration and career development. However, I am a national certified financial educator, Dave Ramsey trained Financial Coach and today I live debt free! Because your situation is fact dependent you may require the assistance of specific, qualified professionals and I encourage you to seek them out.

Since I have been certified as a financial educator, taught personal finance classes and conducted many workshops and seminars, there are a few topics that I often get questions on, but did not find a place in this book to address them. They are relevant questions, so I thought I would share my thoughts with you about the most frequently asked questions or concerns.

My Man Won't Get Involved!

At our classes and seminars over the years, we started to notice that nearly all attendees are women. Single women and married attend about equally. Most of the married women come alone with their spouses uninterested in joining them. The unaccompanied married women frequently ask us what they can do to get their husbands interested and involved. I love it when they ask this.

Bradley was the type of guy that was wishy-washy when it came to our family finances. I was the financially nerdy type who loved balancing the checkbook, keeping an eye on the bank accounts, and who did our annual income taxes. All I had to do was hand him a pen and say "sign here" and whatever I thought should be done with the money was done. Everything was taken care of, or so he thought.

As I mentioned in Chapter 7, I had to drag Bradley, huffing & puffing, to the financial freedom classes. He came very reluctantly. In fact, I think we got into an argument on the way to the first class. I know we argued after the class and even into the next several weeks. My main ammunition was no criticism. I did not beat him over the head or insist that he do anything.

My most successful technique was prayer. I prayed for my husband (still do) to be the man God intended him to be. I prayed for peace in my home. Most importantly I prayed for God to change me. I knew I had issues as a wife, mother, and steward of His resources. I truly believe when I prayed to God to change me was when Bradley began to change. I can't explain how it has happened that in less than 7 years, the same man who wanted nothing to do with our family finances, has been called to take over the financial empowerment space and share with others how they can win. Can you believe it?

I'm not saying this is what will happen to your brother, fiancé, or husband, or in your home. I can only share what worked for me and my house. God has a different plan for each household and if you yield to His voice and power you will see His plan come in time. As a side note: please, if there is abuse in your home, you must get help—immediately!

Sick and Tired

This isn't really about a question that has been asked, but more about the essence of the questions and comments people (especially women) have had about this topic over the years. When I share my story of the sacrifices I made along my Journey to win, I often see faces contort, sighs, and much more. I can immediately tell whether someone is ready to do what it takes to win.

What I can tell you is that until you get to the place when you are sick and tired of living the American nightmare and justifying the bad behavior that has you in the place you are in, you will not win. It was very hard for me to hear that years ago listening to the radio, but it is still the Truth. No one can make you decide to take this journey. No one can keep you committed on this journey. No one can decide what sacrifices you have to make—only you can do that.

When I had completed the courses, passed comprehensive exams and began the dissertation phase for my doctoral degree, I called up my dear friend Dr. Vicki Williams. After hours on the phone explaining to her that I didn't know if I could continue and I was unsure if I could do all that was required of me, she told me, "Bonita, you can do one of two things: you can continue life as you know it and you will be among those who never finish; or you can make sacrifices by kissing your social life good-bye for a season, get the research study done, graduate, and get on with the new life that is waiting for you!"

Those words changed my life. I did sacrifice. I buckled down and carried my laptop everywhere. I turned off the TV and wrote pages upon pages into the nights. I burned lots of midnight oil. The end result was a 250-page dissertation, and the successful defense and graduation that my mother lived to see. If I had dilly-dallied any longer, she would have passed away before I could have finished. I was sick and tired of not having completed my degree, so I made the necessary sacrifices to "get 'er dun."

It took supernatural strength and alignment of people, places and things for us to have accomplished in one year what we could not accomplish in seven. God and his resources were clearly at work complimenting our efforts and commitment to the process. It reminds me of when God commanded Joshua to go take the land that He promised the Israelites. He told Joshua to lead the Army. He would not fail or forsake them and asked them to "be strong and courageous." When we knew what God required of us, that we did. The outcome speaks the truth of our obedience.

You may choose to continue burying your head in the sand doing things halfway while you enjoy and indulge in some of the benefits, and prolonging your victory; or, you can dive in headfirst and quickly get to the other side. How long will it take you to live the new life God has waiting for you? The choice is yours.

Best Regards

The journey is a lifelong journey. It will not stop when you have no creditors to pay. It will not stop when college for your children is partially or fully funded. It will not stop when your mortgage is paid or your retirement fund grows larger. You will have to commit to this process and these principles as long as you manage a household. I wish you the best in your journey. My hope and prayer is that you will share with others what you have learned reading this book. In other words, pay it forward!

References

Miley, M., and Mack, A. (2009). *The New Female Consumer: The Rise of the Real Mom*. A White Paper by Advertising Age.

TheCurrentMoment.com (2011, Nov. 1) *Debt, Rights & Social Goods*. Blog Retrieved May 1, 2013 at http://thecurrentmoment.wordpress.com/2011/11/01/debt-rights-and-social-goods/.

U.S. Bureau of Labor Statistics. (2013, April). *Consumer Expenditures in 2011*. Report #1042.

U.S. Census Bureau. (2012). *Income, Expenditures, Poverty, and Wealth*, p.457.

Washington, G. (2013). *If I Should Die Before I Wake: Life Celebration Planner*. Lulu.com

Resources

Following is a brief list of resources to help you on the journey. Additional information is available at www.ypeconomy.com

Car Valuation Sites:
- Kelly Blue Book – www.kbb.com
- NADA – www.nada.com

Credit Cards, Collections and Scoring:
- The Credit Card Act – http://tinyurl.com/ykskuxz
- FICO scoring – www.myfico.com

Credit Report:
- Annual Credit Report – www.annualcreditreport.com

Credit Bureaus:
- Experian – www.experian.com
- Transunion – www.transunion.com
- Equifax – www.equifax.com

Legacy/Legal Planning:
- US Legal Forms – www.uslegalforms.com
- Zander Insurance – www.zanderins.com
- Legal Zoom – www.legalzoom.com
- If I Should Die Before I Wake Life Celebration Planner – http://tinyurl.com/mmpn65p

Movies:

- Maxed out – www.maxedoutmovie.com
- Debt Slapped – www.debtslapped.org
- In Debt We Trust – http://youtu.be/TVr813HkEjM
- ESPN 30 for 30: Broke – http://tinyurl.com/9qxbg25

Forms

Visit our website, www.ypeconomy.com, to download and print the forms mentioned throughout the book. Instructions are included with each.

- I own/ I owe
- Debt Avalanche
- Basic budget
- Short Term Saving
- Four Walls
- If I Should Die Before I Wake Life Celebration Planner
- * Bonus forms are also available

The Vinsons are trained financial counselors and are certified through the National Financial Educator's Council.

They work with churches, organizations & businesses across the country to deliver the tools of debt-free living through a process, not products.

They are highly sought after for their popular, interactive and entertaining seminars that inspires audiences to break the chains of debt, build wealth and live free of financial stress. Visit **www.YPEconomy.com** for details.

· YOUR PERSONAL ECONOMY · SEMINARS · FINANCIAL EMPOWERMENT COACHING &

YPE

Bradley & Bonita Vinson
Authors, Speakers, Coaches

The Faith-Based Financial Literacy & Education Experts